CW00385756

The Road that Leads to Life

Lent and Easter
with Pope Francis

*All booklets are published thanks to the
generous support of the members of the
Catholic Truth Society*

CATHOLIC TRUTH SOCIETY

PUBLISHERS TO THE HOLY SEE

Contents

All rights reserved. First published 2016 by The Incorporated Catholic Truth Society, 40-46 Harleyford Road London SE11 5AY Tel: 020 7640 0042 Fax: 020 7640 0046. This edition © 2016 The Incorporated Catholic Truth Society, text © 2015 Libreria Editrice Vaticana.

ISBN 978 1 78469 096 0

SEASON OF LENT

Ash Wednesday

Beginning the Lenten journey

As the people of God begin the journey of Lent, the time in which we seek to be more firmly united to the Lord, to share the mystery of his Passion and his Resurrection.

Today's liturgy offers us first and foremost a passage from the prophet Joel, whom God sent to call the people of God to repentance and conversion, due to a natural disaster (a plague of locusts) which was devastating Judea. The Lord alone can save us from the scourge and it is therefore necessary to entreat him with prayer and fasting, confessing one's sins.

The prophet emphasizes interior conversion: "return to me with all your heart" (*Jl* 2:12).

Returning to the Lord "with all your heart" means to begin the journey not of a superficial and transitory conversion, but rather of a spiritual itinerary with regard to the most intimate place of our person. The heart is, indeed, the seat of our feelings, the centre in which our decisions, our attitudes mature. That "return to me with all your heart" involves not only individuals, but is extended to the community as a whole. It is a convocation directed to everyone: "gather the people. Sanctify the congregation;

assemble the elders; gather the children, even nursing infants. Let the bridegroom leave his room, and the bride her chamber" (v. 16). The prophet pauses particularly on the prayer of the priests, pointing out that it is to be accompanied by tears. It will do us good, all of us, but especially for us as priests, at the beginning of Lent, to ask for the gift of tears, so as to render our prayer and our journey of conversion ever more authentic and free from hypocrisy. It will do us good to ask ourselves this question: "Do I weep? Does the Pope weep? Do the cardinals weep? Do bishops weep? Do the consecrated weep? Do priests weep? Is there weeping in our prayers?". And this is precisely the message of today's Gospel. In the passage from Matthew, Jesus again reads the three works of mercy called for by Mosaic law: almsgiving, prayer and fasting. He distinguishes the external disposition from the interior disposition, from the weeping of the heart. Over time, these prescriptions were corroded by external formalism, or they even mutated into a sign of social superiority. Jesus highlighted a common temptation in these three works, that can be summarized precisely as hypocrisy (he mentions it three times): "Beware of practicing your piety before men in order to be seen by them…. When you give alms, sound no trumpet before you, as the hypocrites do…. And when you pray, you must not be like the hypocrites; for they love to stand and pray…that they may be seen by men…. And when you fast, do not look dismal, like the hypocrites…"

(*Mt* 6:1, 2, 5, 16). You know, brothers, that hypocrites do not know how to weep, they have forgotten how to weep, they do not ask for the gift of tears.

Be reconciled to God

When one performs a good work, the desire arises almost instinctively in us to be esteemed and admired for this good action, to gain satisfaction from it. Jesus calls us to perform these gestures without ostentation, and to rely solely on the reward of the Father "who sees in secret" (*Mt* 6:4, 6, 18).

Dear brothers and sisters, the Lord never tires of having mercy on us, and wants to offer us his forgiveness once again - we all need it - inviting us to return to him with a new heart, purified of evil, purified by tears, to take part in his joy. How should we accept this invitation? St Paul advises us: "We beseech you on behalf of Christ, be reconciled to God" (*2 Co* 5:20). This power of conversion is not only the work of mankind, it is letting oneself be reconciled. Reconciliation between us and God is possible thanks to the mercy of the Father who, out of love for us, did not hesitate to sacrifice his only begotten Son. Indeed Christ, who was just and without sin, was made to be sin (cf. v. 21) when, on the Cross, he took on the burden of our sins, and in this way he redeemed and justified us before God. "In him" we can become just, in him we can change, if we accept the grace of God and do not allow this "acceptable time" to pass in vain (*2 Co* 6:2). Please, let us stop, let us stop a while and let ourselves be reconciled to God.

The call to conversion

With this awareness, we begin the Lenten journey with trust and joy. May Immaculate Mother Mary, without sin, sustain our spiritual battle against sin, accompany us at this acceptable time, so that we may come together to sing of the exultant victory on Easter Day. And as a sign of the will to let ourselves be reconciled to God, in addition to the tears that will be "in secret", in public we will perform this gesture of the imposition of Ashes on the head. The celebrant speaks these words: "Remember that you are dust, and to dust you shall return" (cf. *Gn* 3:19); or repeats the exhortation of Jesus: "Repent, and believe in the Gospel" (cf. *Mk* 1:15). Both formulae are a reference to the truth of human existence: we are limited creatures, always sinners in need of repentance and conversion. How important it is to listen to and accept this call in this time of ours! The call to conversion is thus an incentive to return, as the son in the parable did, to the arms of God, gentle and merciful Father, to weep in that embrace, to trust in him and entrust ourselves to him.

First Sunday of Lent
The road that leads to life

Last Wednesday, with the rite of Ashes, Lent began, and today is the First Sunday of this Liturgical Season which refers to the forty days Jesus spent in the desert, after his Baptism in the River Jordan. St Mark writes in today's Gospel: "The Spirit immediately drove him out into the wilderness. And he was in the wilderness forty days, tempted by Satan; and he was with the wild beasts; and the angels ministered to him" (*Mk* 1:12-13). With these simple words the Evangelist describes the trials willingly faced by Jesus before he began his messianic mission. It is a trial from which the Lord leaves victorious and which prepares him to proclaim the Gospel of the Kingdom of God. In these forty days of solitude, he confronts Satan "body to body", he unmasks Satan's temptations and conquers him. And through him, we have all conquered, but we must protect this victory in our daily lives.

The Church reminds us of that mystery at the beginning of Lent, so that it may give us the perspective and the meaning of this time, which is a time of combat. Lent is a *time of combat! A spiritual combat against the spirit of evil* (cf. Collective Prayer for Ash Wednesday). And while we cross the Lenten "desert", we keep our gaze fixed upon Easter, which is the definitive victory of Jesus against the Evil One, against sin and against death. This is the meaning of this First Sunday of Lent: to place ourselves decisively on the path of Jesus, the road that leads to life. To look at Jesus. Look at what Jesus has done and go with him.

The desert

This path of Jesus passes through *the desert*. The desert is the place where *the voice of God and the voice of the tempter* can be heard. In the noise, in the confusion, this cannot be done; only superficial voices can be heard. Instead we can go deeper in the desert, where our destiny is truly played out, life or death. And how do we hear the voice of God? We hear it in his Word. For this reason, it is important to know Scripture, because otherwise we do not know how to react to the snares of the Evil One. And here I would like to return to my advice of reading the Gospel every day. Read the Gospel every day! Meditate on it for a little while, for ten minutes. And also to carry it with you in your pocket or your purse…. But always have the Gospel at hand. The Lenten desert helps us to say 'no' to worldliness, to the "idols", it helps us to make courageous choices in accordance with the Gospel and to strengthen solidarity with the brothers.

Now let us enter into the desert without fear, because we are not alone: we are *with Jesus, with the Father and with the Holy Spirit*. In fact, as it was for Jesus, it is the Holy Spirit who guides us on the Lenten journey; that same *Spirit that descended upon Jesus and that has been given to us in Baptism*.

Lent, therefore is an appropriate time that should lead us to be ever more aware of how much the Holy Spirit, received in Baptism, has worked and can work in us. And at the end of the Lenten itinerary, at the Easter Vigil, we can renew with greater awareness the Baptismal covenant and the commitments that flow from it.

May the Blessed Virgin, model of docility to the Spirit, help us to let ourselves be led by him, who wishes to make each of us a "new creature".

SECOND SUNDAY OF LENT

Love transfigures all

Last Sunday the Liturgy presented Jesus tempted by Satan in the desert, but victorious over temptation. In the light of this Gospel, we are again made aware of our condition as sinners, but also of the victory over evil for those who undertake the journey of conversion and, like Jesus, want to do the Father's will. In this second Sunday of Lent, the Church points out to us *the end* of this journey of conversion, namely participation in *the glory of Christ*, which shines on the face of the obedient Servant, who died and rose for us.

The Gospel page recounts the event of the Transfiguration, which takes place at the height of Jesus' public ministry. He is on his way to Jerusalem, where the prophecies of the "Servant of God" and his redemptive sacrifice are to be fulfilled. The crowds did not understand this: presented with a Messiah who contrasted with their earthly expectations, they abandoned him. They thought the Messiah would be the liberator from Roman domination, the emancipator of the homeland, and they do not like Jesus' perspective and so they leave him. Neither do the Apostles understand the words with which Jesus proclaims the outcome of his mission in the glorious passion, they do not understand! Jesus thus chooses to give to Peter, James and John a foretaste of his glory, which he will have after the Resurrection, in order to confirm them in faith and encourage them to follow him on the trying path, on the Way of the Cross. Thus, on a high mountain, immersed in prayer, he is transfigured before them: his face and his entire person irradiate a blinding light. The three disciples are frightened, as a cloud envelops them and the Father's voice sounds from above, as at the Baptism on the Jordan: "This is my beloved Son; listen to him" (*Mk* 9:7). Jesus is the Son-made-Servant, sent into the world to save us all through the Cross, fulfilling the plan of salvation. His full adherence to God's will renders his *humanity transparent to the glory of God, who is love.*

The radiance of his glory

Jesus thus reveals himself as the perfect icon of the Father, the radiance of his glory. He is the fulfilment of revelation; that is why beside him appear transfigured, Moses and Elijah; they represent the Law and the Prophets, so as to signify that everything finishes and begins in Jesus, in his passion and in his glory.

Their instructions for the disciples and for us is this: "Listen to him!". Listen to Jesus. He is the Saviour: follow him. To listen to Christ, in fact, entails *taking up the logic of his Paschal Mystery*, setting out on the journey with him to make of oneself a gift of love to others, in docile obedience to the will of God, with an attitude of detachment from worldly things and of interior freedom. One must, in other words, be willing to "lose one's very life" (cf. *Mk* 8:35), by giving it up so that all men might be saved: thus, we will meet in eternal happiness. The path to Jesus always leads us to happiness, don't forget it! Jesus' way always leads us to happiness. There will always be a cross, trials in the middle, but at the end we are always led to happiness. Jesus does not deceive us, he promised us happiness and will give it to us if we follow his ways.

With Peter, James and John we too climb the Mount of the Transfiguration today and stop in contemplation of the face of Jesus to retrieve the message and translate it into our lives; for we too can be transfigured by love. In reality, love is capable of transfiguring everything. Love transfigures all! Do you believe this?

THIRD SUNDAY OF LENT

Building for God a temple of our lives

Today's Gospel presents the episode of the expulsion of the merchants from the temple (*Jn* 2:13-25). Jesus made "a whip of cords, he drove them all, with the sheep and oxen, out of the temple" (*Jn* 2:15), the money, everything. Such a gesture gave rise to strong impressions in the people and in the disciples. It clearly appeared as a prophetic gesture, so much so that some of those present asked Jesus: "What sign have you to show us for doing this?" (v. 18), who are you to do these things? Show us a sign that you have authority to do them. They were seeking a divine and prodigious sign that would confirm that Jesus was sent by God. And he responded: "Destroy this temple, and in three days I will raise it up" (v. 19). They replied: "It has taken forty-six years to build this temple, and you will raise it up in three days?" (v. 20). They did not understand that the Lord was referring to the living temple of his body, that would be destroyed in the death on the Cross, but would be raised on the third day. Thus, in three days. "When therefore he was raised from the dead, his disciples remembered that he had said this; and they believed the Scripture and the word Jesus had spoken" (v. 22).

In effect, this gesture of Jesus and his prophetic message are fully understood in the light of his Paschal Mystery. We have here, according to the evangelist John, the first proclamation of the death and resurrection of Christ: his body, destroyed on the Cross by the violence of sin, will become in the Resurrection the universal meeting place between God and mankind. And the Risen Christ is himself the universal meeting place - for everyone! - between God and mankind. For this reason, his humanity is the true temple where God is revealed, speaks, is encountered; and the true worshippers, the true worshippers of God are not only the guardians of the material temple, the keepers of power and of religious knowledge, [but] they are those who worship God "in spirit and truth" (*Jn* 4:23).

His way of cleansing

In this time of Lent we are preparing for the celebration of Easter, when we will renew the promises of our Baptism. Let us walk in the world as Jesus did, and let us make our whole existence a sign of our love for our brothers, especially the weakest and poorest, let us build for God a temple of our lives. And so we make it "encounterable" for those who we find along our journey. If we are witnesses of the Living Christ, so many people will encounter Jesus in us, in our witness. But, we ask - and each one of us can ask ourselves - does the Lord feel at home in my life? Do we allow him to "cleanse" our hearts and to drive out the idols, those attitudes of cupidity, jealousy, worldliness, envy, hatred, those habits of gossiping and tearing down others. Do I allow him to cleanse all the behaviours that are against God, against our neighbour, and against ourselves, as we heard today in the first Reading? Each one can answer for himself or herself, in the silence of his or her heart: "Do I allow Jesus to make my heart a little cleaner?" "Oh Father, I fear the rod!" But Jesus never strikes. Jesus cleanses with tenderness, mercy, love. Mercy is his way of cleansing. Let us, each of us, let us allow the Lord to enter with his mercy - not with the whip, no, with his mercy - to cleanse our hearts. With us, Jesus' whip is his mercy. Let us open to him the gates so that he will make us a little purer.

Every Eucharist that we celebrate with faith makes us grow as a living temple of the Lord, thanks to the communion with his crucified and risen Body. Jesus recognizes what is in each of us, and knows well our most ardent desires: that of being inhabited by him, only by him. Let us allow him to enter into our lives, into our families, into our hearts. May Mary most holy, the privileged dwelling place of the Son of God, accompany us and sustain us on the Lenten journey, so that we might be able to rediscover the beauty of the encounter with Christ, the only One who frees us and saves us.

Today's Gospel

In the Gospel passage that we heard, there are two things that strike me: an image and a word. The image is that of Jesus, with whip in hand, driving out all those who took advantage of the Temple to do business. These profiteers who sold animals for sacrifices, changed coins…. There was the sacred - the Temple, sacred - and this filth, outside. This is the image. And Jesus takes the whip and goes forth, to somewhat cleanse the Temple.

And the phrase, the word, is there where it says that so many people believe in him, a horrible phrase: "but Jesus did not trust himself to them, because he knew all men and needed no one to bear witness of man; for he himself knew what was in man" (*Jn* 2:24-25).

We cannot deceive Jesus. He knows us from within. He did not trust them. He, Jesus did not trust them. And this can be a fine mid-Lenten question: Can Jesus trust himself to me? Can Jesus trust me, or am I two-faced? Do I play the Catholic, one close to the Church, and then live as a pagan? "But Jesus doesn't know, no one goes and tells him about it". He knows. "He needed no one to bear witness; indeed, he knew what was in man". Jesus knows all that there is in our heart. We cannot deceive Jesus. In front of him, we cannot pretend to be saints, and close our eyes, act like this, and then live a life that is not what he wants. And he knows. And we all know the name he gave to those who had two faces: hypocrites.

It will do us good today, to enter our hearts and look at Jesus. To say to him: "Lord, look, there are good things, but there are also things that aren't good. Jesus, do you trust me? I am a sinner…". This doesn't scare Jesus. If you tell him: "I'm a sinner", it doesn't scare him. What distances him is one who is two-faced: showing himself or herself as just in order to cover up hidden sin. "But I go to Church, every Sunday, and I…". Yes, we can say all of this. But if your heart isn't just, if you don't do justice, if you don't love those who need love, if you do not live according to the spirit of the Beatitudes, you are not Catholic. You are a hypocrite. First: can Jesus trust himself to me? In prayer, let us ask him: Lord, do you trust me?

To cleanse your soul

Second, the gesture. When we enter our hearts, we find things that aren't okay, things that aren't good, as Jesus found that filth of profiteering, of the profiteers, in the Temple. Inside of us too, there are unclean things, there are sins of selfishness, of arrogance, pride, greed, envy, jealousy…so many sins! We can even continue the dialogue with Jesus: "Jesus, do you trust me? I want you to trust me. Thus I open the door to you, and you cleanse my soul". Ask the Lord that, as he went to cleanse the Temple, he may come to cleanse your soul. We imagine that he comes with a whip of cords…. No, he doesn't cleanse the soul with that! Do you know what kind of whip Jesus uses to cleanse our soul? Mercy. Open your heart to Jesus' mercy! Say: "Jesus, look how much filth! Come, cleanse. Cleanse with your mercy, with your tender words, cleanse with your caresses". If we open our heart to Jesus' mercy, in order to cleanse our heart, our soul, Jesus will trust himself to us.

Penitential Celebration
Rich in mercy

This year again, on the eve of the Fourth Sunday of Lent, we are gathered to celebrate the penitential liturgy. We are united with the many Christians who, today, in every part of the world, have accepted the invitation to live this moment as a sign of the Lord's goodness. The Sacrament of Reconciliation, indeed, allows us to draw near to the Father with trust to have the certainty of his forgiveness. He is truly "rich in mercy" and extends it abundantly upon those who appeal to him with a sincere heart.

Being here to experience his love, in any case, is above all a fruit of his grace. As the Apostle Paul reminded us, God never ceases to demonstrate the wealth of his mercy throughout the centuries. The transformation of the heart that leads us to confess our sins is a "gift from God". We cannot do it alone. The power to confess our sins is a gift from God, it is a gift, it is "his work" (cf. *Ep* 2:8-10). Being touched with tenderness by his hand and moulded by his grace allows us to draw near to the priest without fear for our sins, but with the certainty that we will be accepted by him in the name of God, and understood despite our wretchedness; and even to approach without a defence attorney: we have the One who alone gave his life for our sins! It is he who always defends us before the Father, he always defends us. As we exit the confessional, we will feel his strength which gives new life and restores ardour to the faith. After confession we are reborn.

Love and judgement

The Gospel we have heard (cf. *Lk* 7:36-50) opens to us a path of hope and comfort. It is good to feel Jesus' compassionate gaze upon us, just as it was felt by the sinful woman in the house of the Pharisee. In this passage two words persistently return: love and judgement.

There is the love of the sinful woman who humbles herself before the Lord; but before that is the merciful love of Jesus for her, which drives her to approach him. Her tears of repentance and joy wash the feet of the Master, and her hair dries them with gratitude; the kisses are an expression of her pure love; and the perfumed ointment poured in abundance attests to how precious he is in her eyes. This woman's every gesture speaks of love and expresses her desire to have unwavering certitude in her life: that of having been forgiven. And this certitude is beautiful! And Jesus gives her this certitude: in accepting her he demonstrates the love God has for her, just for her, a public sinner! Love and forgiveness are simultaneous: God forgives her many sins, he forgives her for all of them, for "she loved much" (*Lk* 7:47); and she adores Jesus because she feels that in him there is mercy and not condemnation. She feels that Jesus understands her with love, she who is a sinner. Thanks to Jesus, God lifts her many sins off her shoulders, he no longer remembers them (cf. *Is* 43:25). For this is also true: when God forgives, he forgets. God's forgiveness is great! For her now a new era begins; through love she is reborn into a new life.

This woman has truly encountered the Lord. In silence, she opened her heart; in sorrow, she showed repentance for her sins; by her tears, she appealed to divine goodness to receive forgiveness. For her there will be no judgement but that which comes from God, and this is the judgement of mercy. The hero of this encounter is certainly love, a mercy which goes beyond justice.

Called to look beyond

Simon, the master of the house, the Pharisee, on the contrary, doesn't manage to find the road of love. Everything is calculated, everything is thought out…. He stands firm on the threshold of formality. It is an unpleasant thing, formal love, he doesn't understand. He is not capable of taking that next step forward to meet Jesus who will bring him salvation. Simon limits himself to inviting Jesus to lunch, but did not truly welcome him. In his thoughts Simon invokes only justice and in doing so he errs. His judgement of the woman distances him from the truth and prevents him from even understanding who his guest is. He stopped at the surface - at formality - incapable of seeing the heart. Before the parable of Jesus and the question of which servant would love more, the Pharisee responds correctly: "The one, I suppose, to whom he forgave more". Jesus doesn't fail to observe: "You have judged rightly" (*Lk* 7:43). When Simon's judgement is turned to love, then is he in the right.

Jesus' reminder urges each of us never to stop at the surface of things, especially when we have a person before us. We are called to look beyond, to focus on the heart in order to see how much generosity everyone is capable of. No one can be excluded from the mercy of God; everyone knows the way to access it and the Church is the house where everyone is welcomed and no one is rejected. Her doors remain wide open, so that those who are touched by grace may find the assurance of forgiveness. The greater the sin, the greater the love that must be shown by the Church to those who repent. With how much love Jesus looks at us! With how much love he heals our sinful heart! Our sins never scare him. Let us consider the prodigal son who, when he decided to return to his father, considers making a speech, but the father doesn't let him speak. He embraces him (cf. *Lk* 15:17-24). This is the way Jesus is with us. "Father, I have so many sins….." - "But he will be glad if you go: he will embrace you with such love! Don't be afraid".

Fourth Sunday of Lent

God so loved the world

Today's Gospel again offers us the words that Jesus addressed to Nicodemus: "For God so loved the world that he gave his only Son" (*Jn* 3:16). In hearing these words, we turn our heart's gaze to Jesus Crucified and we feel within us that God loves us, truly loves us, and he loves us so much! This is the simplest expression that epitomizes all of the Gospel, all of the faith, all of theology: *God loves us with a free and boundless love.*

This is how God loves us and God shows this love first through *creation*, as the Liturgy announces, in the fourth Eucharistic Prayer: "You have created all things, to fill your creatures with every blessing and lead all men to the joyful vision of your light". At the beginning of the world there is only the freely given love of the Father. St Irenaeus, a saint of the first centuries, writes: "In the beginning, therefore, did God form Adam, not as if he stood in need of man, but that he might have one upon whom to confer his benefits" (*Adversus Haereses*, IV, 14, 1). It is like this, God's love is like this.

Thus the fourth Eucharistic Prayer continues: "Even when he disobeyed you and lost your friendship you did not abandon him to the power of death", but with your mercy "helped all men to seek and find you". He came with his mercy. As in creation, and also in the subsequent stages of salvation history, the freely given love of God returns: the Lord *chooses his people* not because they are deserving but because *they are the smallest among all peoples*, as he says. And when "the fullness of time" arrived, despite the fact that man had repeatedly broken the covenant, God, rather than abandoning him, formed a new bond with him, in the blood of Jesus - the bond of a new and everlasting covenant - a bond that nothing will ever break.

God, who is rich in mercy

St Paul reminds us: "God, who is rich in mercy", - never forget that he is rich in mercy - "out of the great love with which he loved us, even when we were dead through our trespasses, made us alive together with Christ" (*Ep* 2:4). The *Cross of Christ* is the supreme proof of the mercy and love that God has for us: Jesus loved us "*to the end*" (*Jn* 13:1), meaning not only to the last instant of his earthly life, but to the farthest limit of love. While in creation the Father gave us proof of his immense love by giving us life, in the passion and death of his Son he gave us the proof of proofs: he came to suffer and die for us. So great is God's mercy: he loves us, he forgives us; God forgives all and God forgives always.

May Mary, who is the Mother of Mercy, place in our hearts the certitude that we are *loved by God*. May she be close to us in moments of difficulty and give us the sentiments of her Son, so our Lenten journey may be an experience of forgiveness, of welcome, and of charity.

FIFTH SUNDAY OF LENT

Gospel, Crucifix, Witness

On this Fifth Sunday of Lent, John the Evangelist draws our attention with a curious detail: some "Greeks", of the Jewish religion, who have come to Jerusalem for the feast of Passover, turn to Philip and say to him: "We wish to see Jesus" (*Jn* 12:21). There are many people in the holy city, where Jesus has come for the last time, there are many people. There are the little ones and the simple ones, who have warmly welcomed the Prophet of Nazareth, recognizing him as the Messenger of the Lord. There are the High Priests and the leaders of the people, who want to eliminate him because they consider him a heretic and dangerous. There are also people, like those "Greeks", who are curious to see him and to know more about his person and about the works he has performed, the last of which - the resurrection of Lazarus - has caused quite a stir.

"We wish to see Jesus": these words, like so many others in the Gospels, go beyond this particular episode and express something universal; they reveal a desire that passes through the ages and cultures, a desire present in the heart of so many people who have heard of Christ, but have not yet encountered him. "I wish to see Jesus", thus he feels the heart of these people.

Responding indirectly, in a prophetic way, to that request to be able to see him, Jesus pronounces a prophecy that reveals his identity and shows the path to know him truly: "The hour has come for the Son of Man to be glorified" (*Jn* 12:23). It is the hour of the Cross! It is the time for the defeat of Satan, prince of evil, and of the definitive triumph of the merciful love of God. Christ declares that he will be "lifted up from the earth" (v. 32), an expression with a twofold meaning: "lifted" because he is crucified, and "lifted" because he is exalted by the Father in the Resurrection, to draw everyone to him and to reconcile mankind with God and among themselves. The hour of the Cross, the darkest in history, is also the source of salvation for those who believe in him.

Grains of wheat

Continuing in his prophecy of the imminent Passover, Jesus uses a simple and suggestive image, that of the "grain of wheat" that, once fallen into the earth, dies in order to bear fruit (cf. v. 24). In this image we find another aspect of the Cross of Christ: that of fruitfulness. The death of Jesus, in fact, is an inexhaustible source of new life, because it carries within itself the regenerative strength of God's love. Immersed in this love through Baptism, Christians can become "grains of wheat" and bear much fruit if they, like Jesus, "lose their life" out of love for God and brothers and sisters (cf. v. 25).

For this reason, to those who, today too, "wish to see Jesus", to those who are searching for the face of God; to those who received catechesis when they were little and then developed it no further and perhaps have lost their faith; to so many who have not yet encountered Jesus personally…; to all these people we can offer three things: the Gospel, the Crucifix and the witness of our faith, poor but sincere. The Gospel: there we can encounter Jesus, listen to him, know him. The Crucifix: the sign of the love of Jesus who gave himself for us. And then a faith that is expressed in simple gestures of fraternal charity. But mainly in the coherence of life, between what we say and what we do. Coherence between our faith and our life, between our words and our actions: Gospel, Crucifix, Witness.

May Our Lady help us to bring these three things forth.

HOLY WEEK AND THE TRIDUUM

PALM SUNDAY

He humbled himself

At the heart of this celebration, which seems so festive, are the words we heard in the hymn of the Letter to the Philippians: "He humbled himself" (*Ph* 2:8). Jesus' humiliation.

These words show us God's way and, consequently, that which must be the way of Christians: it is humility. A way which constantly amazes and disturbs us: we will never get used to a humble God!

Humility is above all God's way: God humbles himself to walk with his people, to put up with their infidelity. This is clear when we read the story of Exodus. How humiliating for the Lord to hear all that grumbling, all those complaints against Moses, but ultimately against him, their Father, who brought them out of slavery and was leading them on the journey through the desert to the land of freedom.

This week, Holy Week, which leads us to Easter, we will take this path of Jesus' own humiliation. Only in this way will this week be "holy" for us too!

We will feel the contempt of the leaders of his people and their attempts to trip him up. We will be there at the betrayal of Judas, one of the Twelve, who will sell him for thirty pieces of silver. We will see the Lord arrested and carried off like a criminal; abandoned by his disciples, dragged before the Sanhedrin, condemned to death, beaten and insulted. We will hear Peter, the "rock" among the disciples, deny him three times. We will hear the shouts of the crowd, egged on by their leaders, who demand that Barabas be freed and Jesus crucified. We will see him mocked by the soldiers, robed in purple and crowned with thorns. And then, as he makes his sorrowful way beneath the cross, we will hear the jeering of the people and their leaders, who scoff at his being King and Son of God

No humility without humiliation

This is God's way, the way of humility. It is the way of Jesus; there is no other. And there can be no humility without humiliation.

Following this path to the full, the Son of God took on the "form of a slave" (cf. *Ph* 2:7). In the end, humility also means service. It means making room for God by stripping oneself, "emptying oneself", as Scripture says (v. 7). This - the pouring out of oneself - is the greatest humiliation of all.

There is another way, however, opposed to the way of Christ. It is worldliness, the way of the world. The world proposes the way of vanity, pride, success… the other way. The Evil One proposed this way to Jesus too, during his forty days in the desert. But Jesus immediately rejected it. With him, and only by his grace, with his help, we too can overcome this temptation to vanity, to worldliness, not only at significant moments, but in daily life as well.

In this, we are helped and comforted by the example of so many men and women who, in silence and hiddenness, sacrifice themselves daily to serve others: a sick relative, an elderly person living alone, a disabled person, the homeless…

The path of humility

We think too of the humiliation endured by all those who, for their lives of fidelity to the Gospel, encounter discrimination and pay a personal price. We think too of our brothers and sisters who are persecuted because they are Christians, the martyrs of our own time - and there are many. They refuse to deny Jesus and they endure insult and injury with dignity. They follow him on his way. In truth, we can speak of a "cloud of witnesses" - the martyrs of our own time (cf. *Heb* 12:1).

During this week, let us set about with determination along this same path of humility, with immense love for him, our Lord and Saviour. Love will guide us and give us strength. For where he is, we too shall be (cf. *Jn* 12:26).

Wednesday of Holy Week
Meditation on the Triduum

Tomorrow is Holy Thursday. In the afternoon, with the Mass of the Lord's Supper, we will begin the *Easter Triduum* of Christ's passion, death and resurrection, which is the culmination of the whole liturgical year and the pinnacle of our Christian life as well.

The Triduum begins with the commemoration of the Last Supper. Jesus, on the eve of his passion, offered his body and blood to the Father under the species of bread and wine and, which he gave to the Apostles as nourishment with the command that they perpetuate the offering in his memory. The Gospel of this celebration, recalling the *washing of the feet*, expresses the same meaning of the Eucharist under another perspective. Jesus - like a servant - washes the feet of Simon Peter and the other eleven disciples (cf. *Jn* 13:4-5). By this prophetic gesture, he expresses the meaning of his life and of his passion as service to God and to his brothers: "For the Son of man also came not to be served but to serve" (*Mk* 10:45).

This also occurred in our Baptism, when the grace of God washed us of sin and clothed us in Christ's nature (cf. *Col* 3:10). This takes place every time we celebrate the memory of the Lord in the Eucharist: we enter into communion with Christ Servant by obeying his command - to love one another as he has loved us (cf. *Jn* 13:34; 15:12). If we approach Holy Communion without being sincerely ready to wash the feet of one another, we don't recognize the Body of the Lord. It is the service, Jesus gives himself entirely.

The greatest love

Then, the day after tomorrow, in the liturgy of *Good Friday* we shall meditate on the mystery of Christ's death and adore the Cross. In the final moments of his life, before giving up his spirit to the Father, Jesus said: "It is finished" (*Jn* 19:30). What do these words mean, when Jesus says: "It is finished"? It means that the work of salvation is finished, that all of the Scriptures have found their total fulfilment in the love of Christ, the immolated Lamb. Jesus, by his Sacrifice, has transformed the greatest iniquity into the greatest love.

Over the course of the centuries there have been men and women who by the witness of their lives reflected a ray of this perfect love, full and undefiled. I would like to recall a heroic witness of our times, Don Andrea Santoro, a priest of the Diocese of Rome and a missionary in Turkey. A few days before being assassinated in Trebisonda, he wrote: "I live among these people so that Jesus can live among them through me…only by offering one's flesh is salvation possible. The evil that stalks the world must be borne and pain must be shared till the end in one's own flesh as Jesus did" (A. Polselli, *Don Andrea Santoro, le eredità*, Città Nuova, Rome 2008, p. 31). May the example of a man of our times, and so many others, sustain us in the offering of our own life as a gift of love to our brothers and sisters, in the imitation of Jesus.

And today too there are many men and women, true martyrs who offer up their lives with Jesus in order to confess the faith, for this motive alone. It is a service, the service of Christian witness even to the pouring out of blood, a service that Christ rendered for us: he redeemed us to the very end. And this is the meaning of those words "It is finished". How beautiful it will be when we all, at the end of our lives, with our errors and our faults, as well as our good deeds and our love of neighbour, can say to the Father as Jesus did: "It is finished"; not with the kind of perfection with which he said it, but to say: "Lord, I did everything that I could do. It is finished". Adoring the Cross, looking to Jesus, let us think of love, of service, of our lives, of the Christian martyrs, and it will do us good too to think of the end of our lives. No one knows when that will be, but we can ask for the grace to be able to say: "Father, I did what I could do. It is finished".

Something begins in the deepest darkness

Holy Saturday is the day on which the Church contemplates the "repose" of Christ in the sepulchre after the victorious battle of the Cross. On Holy Saturday the Church, yet again, identifies with Mary: all the Church's faith is gathered in her, the first and perfect disciple, the first and perfect believer. In the darkness that enveloped creation, she alone stayed to keep the flame of faith burning, hoping against all hope (cf. *Rm* 4:18) in the Resurrection of Jesus.

And on the great *Easter Vigil*, in which the *Alleluia* resounds once more, we celebrate Christ Risen, the centre and the purpose of the cosmos and of history; we keep vigil filled with hope in expectation of his coming return, when Easter will be fully manifest. At times the dark of night seems to penetrate the soul; at times we think: "there is nothing more to be done", and the heart no longer finds the strength to love…. But it is precisely in the darkness that Christ lights the fire of God's love: a flash breaks through the darkness and announces a new start, something begins in the deepest darkness. We know that the night is "most night like" just before the dawn. In that very darkness Christ conquers and rekindles the fire of love. The stone of sorrow is rolled away leaving room for hope. Behold the great mystery of Easter! On this holy night the Church gives us the light of the Risen One, that in us there will not be the regret of the one who says: "if only…", but the hope of the one who *opens himself to a present filled with future*: Christ has conquered death, and we are with him. Our life does not end at the stone of the sepulchre, our life goes beyond with hope in Christ who is Risen from that very tomb. As Christians we are called to be sentinels of the dawn, who can discern the signs of the Risen One, as did the women and the disciples who ran to the tomb at dawn on the first day of the week.

Dear brothers and sisters, during these days of the Holy Triduum let us not limit ourselves to commemorating the passion of the Lord, but *let us enter into the mystery*, making his feelings and thoughts our own, as the Apostle Paul invites us to do: "Have this mind among yourselves, which is yours in Christ Jesus (*Ph* 2:5). Then ours will be a "Happy Easter".

MASS OF CHRISM

The Lord washes us and cleanses us

"My hand shall ever abide with him, my arms also shall strengthen him" (*Ps* 89:21).

This is what the Lord means when he says: "I have found David, my servant; with my holy oil I have anointed him" (v. 20). It is also what our Father thinks whenever he "encounters" a priest. And he goes on to say: "My faithfulness and my steadfast love shall be with him… He shall cry to me, 'You are my Father, my God and the rock of my salvation'" (vv. 24, 26).

It is good to enter with the Psalmist into this monologue of our God. He is talking about us, his priests, his pastors. But it is not really a monologue, since he is not the only one speaking. The Father says to Jesus: "Your friends, those who love you, can say to me in a particular way: 'You are my Father'" (cf. *Jn* 14:21). If the Lord is so concerned about helping us, it is because he knows that the task of anointing his faithful people is not easy, it is demanding; it can tire us. We experience this in so many ways: from the ordinary fatigue brought on by our daily apostolate to the weariness of sickness, death and even martyrdom.

Our weariness

The tiredness of priests! Do you know how often I think about this weariness which all of you experience? I think about it and I pray about it, often, especially when I am tired myself. I pray for you as you labour amid the people of God entrusted to your care, many of you in lonely and dangerous places. Our weariness, dear priests, is like incense which silently rises up to heaven (cf. *Ps* 141:2; *Rv* 8:3-4). Our weariness goes straight to the heart of the Father.

Know that the Blessed Virgin Mary is well aware of this tiredness and she brings it straight to the Lord. As our Mother, she knows when her children are weary, and this is her greatest concern. "Welcome! Rest, my child. We will speak afterwards…". "Whenever we draw near to her, she says to us: "Am I not here with you, I who am your Mother?" (cf. *Evangelii Gaudium*, 286). And to her Son she will say, as she did at Cana, "They have no wine" (*Jn* 2:3).

It can also happen that, whenever we feel weighed down by pastoral work, we can be tempted to rest however we please, as if rest were not itself a gift of God. We must not fall into this temptation. Our weariness is precious in the eyes of Jesus who embraces us and lifts us up. "Come to me, all who labour and are overburdened, and I will give you rest" (*Mt* 11:28). Whenever a priest feels dead tired, yet is able to bow down in adoration and say: "Enough for today Lord", and entrust himself to the Father, he knows that he will not fall but be renewed. The one who anoints God's faithful people with oil is also himself anointed by the Lord: "He gives you a garland instead of ashes, the oil of gladness instead of mourning, the mantle of praise instead of a faint spirit" (cf. *Is* 61:3).

Learn how to rest!

Let us never forget that a key to fruitful priestly ministry lies in how we rest and in how we look at the way the Lord deals with our weariness. How difficult it is to learn how to rest! This says much about our trust and our ability to realize that that we too are sheep: we need the help of the Shepherd. A few questions can help us in this regard.

Do I know how to rest by accepting the love, gratitude and affection which I receive from God's faithful people? Or, once my pastoral work is done, do I seek more refined relaxations, not those of the poor but those provided by a consumerist society? Is the Holy Spirit truly "rest in times of weariness" for me, or is he just someone who keeps me busy? Do I know how to seek help from a wise priest? Do I know how to take a break from myself, from the demands I make on myself, from my self-seeking and from my self-absorption? Do I know how to spend time with Jesus, with the Father, with the Virgin Mary and Saint Joseph, with my patron saints, and to find rest in their demands, which are easy and light, and in their pleasures, for they delight to be in my company, and in their concerns and standards, which have only to do with the greater glory of God? Do I know how to rest from my enemies under the Lord's protection? Am I preoccupied with how I should speak and act, or do I entrust myself to the Holy Spirit, who will teach me what I need to say in every situation? Do I worry needlessly, or, like Paul, do I find repose by saying: "I know him in whom I have placed my trust" (2 *Tm* 1:12)?

The heart of the shepherd

Let us return for a moment to what today's liturgy describes as the work of the priest: to bring good news to the poor, to proclaim freedom to prisoners and healing to the blind, to offer liberation to the downtrodden and to announce the year of the Lord's favour. Isaiah also mentions consoling the broken-hearted and comforting the afflicted.

These are not easy or purely mechanical jobs, like running an office, building a parish hall or laying out a soccer field for the young of the parish… The tasks of which Jesus speaks call for the ability to show compassion; our hearts are to be "moved" and fully engaged in carrying them out. We are to rejoice with couples who marry; we are to laugh with the children brought to the baptismal font; we are to accompany young fiancés and families; we are to suffer with those who receive the anointing of the sick in their hospital beds; we are to mourn with those burying a loved one… All these emotions…if we do not have an open heart, can exhaust the heart of a shepherd.

For us priests, what happens in the lives of our people is not like a news bulletin: we know our people, we sense what is going on in their hearts. Our own heart, sharing in their suffering, feels "com-passion", is exhausted, broken into a thousand pieces, moved and even "consumed" by the people. Take this, eat this... These are the words the priest of Jesus whispers repeatedly while caring for his faithful people: Take this, eat this; take this, drink this... In this way our priestly life is given over in service, in closeness to the people of God... and this always leaves us weary.

Forms of weariness

I wish to share with you some forms of weariness on which I have meditated.

There is what we can call "the weariness of people, the weariness of the crowd". For the Lord, and for us, this can be exhausting - so the Gospel tells us - yet it is a good weariness, a fruitful and joyful exhaustion. The people who followed Jesus, the families which brought their children to him to be blessed, those who had been cured, those who came with their friends, the young people who were so excited about the Master...they did not even leave him time to eat. But the Lord never tired of being with people. On the contrary, he seemed renewed by their presence (cf. *Evangelii Gaudium*, 11). This weariness in the midst of activity is a grace on which all priests can draw (cf. ibid., 279). And how beautiful it is! People love their priests, they

want and need their shepherds! The faithful never leave us
without something to do, unless we hide in our offices or
go out in our cars wearing sun glasses. There is a good
and healthy tiredness. It is the exhaustion of the priest who
wears the smell of the sheep…but also smiles the smile of
a father rejoicing in his children or grandchildren. It has
nothing to do with those who wear expensive cologne and
who look at others from afar and from above (cf. ibid., 97).
We are the friends of the Bridegroom: this is our joy. If
Jesus is shepherding the flock in our midst, we cannot be
shepherds who are glum, plaintive or, even worse, bored.
The smell of the sheep and the smile of a father…. Weary,
yes, but with the joy of those who hear the Lord saying:
"Come, O blessed of my Father" (*Mt* 25:34).

There is also the kind of weariness which we can call
"the weariness of enemies". The devil and his minions
never sleep and, since their ears cannot bear to hear the
word of God, they work tirelessly to silence that word
and to distort it. Confronting them is more wearying. It
involves not only doing good, with all the exertion this
entails, but also defending the flock and oneself from evil
(cf. *Evangelii Gaudium*, 83). The evil one is far more astute
than we are, and he is able to demolish in a moment what
it took us years of patience to build up. Here we need to
implore the grace to learn how to "offset" (and it is an
important habit to acquire): to thwart evil without pulling
up the good wheat, or presuming to protect like supermen

what the Lord alone can protect. All this helps us not to let our guard down before the depths of iniquity, before the mockery of the wicked. In these situations of weariness, the Lord says to us: "Have courage! I have overcome the world!" (*Jn* 16:33). The word of God gives us strength.

Only love gives true rest

And finally - I say finally lest you be too wearied by this homily itself! - there is also "weariness of ourselves" (cf. *Evangelii Gaudium*, 277). This may be the most dangerous weariness of all. That is because the other two kinds come from being exposed, from going out of ourselves to anoint and to do battle (for our job is to care for others). But this third kind of weariness is more "self-referential": it is dissatisfaction with oneself, but not the dissatisfaction of someone who directly confronts himself and serenely acknowledges his sinfulness and his need for God's mercy, his help; such people ask for help and then move forward. Here we are speaking of a weariness associated with "wanting yet not wanting", having given up everything but continuing to yearn for the fleshpots of Egypt, toying with the illusion of being something different. I like to call this kind of weariness "flirting with spiritual worldliness". When we are alone, we realize how many areas of our life are steeped in this worldliness, so much so that we may feel that it can never be completely washed away. This can be a dangerous kind of weariness. The Book of Revelation shows us the reason for this weariness: "You have borne up for my sake and you have not grown weary. But I have this against you, that you have abandoned the love you had at first" (*Rv* 2:3-4). Only love gives true rest. What is not loved becomes tiresome, and in time, brings about a harmful weariness.

The most profound and mysterious image of how the Lord deals with our pastoral tiredness is that, "having loved his own, he loved them to the end" (*Jn* 13:1): the scene of his washing the feet of his disciples. I like to think of this as the cleansing of discipleship. The Lord purifies the path of discipleship itself. He "gets involved" with us (*Evangelii Gaudium*, 24), becomes personally responsible for removing every stain, all that grimy, worldly smog which clings to us from the journey we make in his name.

The Lord washes away the grime of our labours

From our feet, we can tell how the rest of our body is doing. The way we follow the Lord reveals how our heart is faring. The wounds on our feet, our sprains and our weariness, are signs of how we have followed him, of the paths we have taken in seeking the lost sheep and in leading the flock to green pastures and still waters (cf. ibid., 270). The Lord washes us and cleanses us of all the dirt our feet have accumulated in following him. This is something holy. Do not let your feet remain dirty. Like battle wounds, the Lord kisses them and washes away the grime of our labours.

Our discipleship itself is cleansed by Jesus, so that we can rightly feel "joyful", "fulfilled", "free of fear and guilt", and impelled to go out "even to the ends of the earth, to every periphery". In this way we can bring the good news to the most abandoned, knowing that "he is with us always, even to the end of the world". And please, let us ask for the grace to learn how to be weary, but weary in the best of ways!

HOLY THURSDAY, MASS OF THE LORD'S SUPPER

He became a slave to serve us

On this Thursday, Jesus was at table with the disciples, celebrating the feast of Passover. And the passage of the Gospel which we heard contains a phrase that is the very core of what Jesus did for us: "having loved his own who were in the world, he loved them to the end" (*Jn* 13:1). Jesus loved us. Jesus loves us. Without limit, always, to the end. Jesus' love for us knows no limits: always more and more. He never tires of loving anyone. He loves us all, to the point of giving his life for us. Yes, giving his life for us; yes, giving his life for all of us, giving his life for each one of us. And every one of us can say: "He gave his life for me". Everyone: he gave his life for you, for you, for you, for you, for me, for him…[pointing to the inmates] for each person, by first and last name. His love is like that: personal. Jesus' love never disappoints, because he never tires of loving, just as he never tires of forgiving, never tires of embracing us. This is the first thing that I wanted to say to you: Jesus loved us, every one of us, to the end.

And then, he does something that the disciples don't understand: washing the feet. In that time, this was usual, it was customary, because when the people arrived in a home, their feet were dirty with the dust of the road; there were no cobblestones at that time.... There were dusty roads. And at the entrance to the house, they washed their feet. It was not done by the master of the house but by the slaves. That was the task of a slave. And like a slave, Jesus washes our feet, the feet of his disciples, and that is why he says: "What I am doing you do not know now, but afterward you will understand" (*Jn* 13:7). Jesus' love is so great that he became a slave to serve us, to heal us, to cleanse us.

Becoming a better servant

Today, in this Mass, the Church would like the priest to wash the feet of twelve people, in memory of the twelve Apostles. But in our hearts we must be certain, we must be sure that, when the Lord washes our feet, he washes us entirely, he purifies us, he lets us feel his love yet again. There is a very beautiful phrase in the Bible, the prophet Isaiah says: "Can a mother forget her child? But even if a mother could forget her child, I will never forget you" (cf. 49:15). God's love for us is like this.

And today I will wash the feet of twelve of you, but all of you are in these brothers and sisters, all of you, everyone. Everyone who lives here. You represent them.

But I too need to be washed by the Lord, and for this you pray during the Mass, that the Lord also wash away my impurities, that I might become a better servant to you, a better slave at the service of the people, as Jesus was.

PASCHAL VIGIL, HOLY SATURDAY
Entering into the mystery

Tonight is a night of vigil. The Lord is not sleeping; the Watchman is watching over his people (cf. *Ps* 121:4), to bring them out of slavery and to open before them the way to freedom.

The Lord is keeping watch and, by the power of his love, he is bringing his people through the Red Sea. He is also bringing Jesus through the abyss of death and the netherworld.

This was a night of vigil for the disciples of Jesus, a night of sadness and fear. The men remained locked in the Upper Room. Yet, the women went to the tomb at dawn on Sunday to anoint Jesus' body. Their hearts were overwhelmed and they were asking themselves: "How will we enter? Who will roll back the stone of the tomb?…" But here was the first sign of the great event: the large stone was already rolled back and the tomb was open!

"Entering the tomb, they saw a young man sitting on the right side, dressed in a white robe…" (*Mk* 16:5). The women were the first to see this great sign, the empty tomb; and they were the first to enter…

"Entering the tomb". It is good for us, on this Vigil night, to reflect on the experience of the women, which also speaks to us. For that is why we are here: to enter, to enter into the Mystery which God has accomplished with his vigil of love.

Amid the great silence

We cannot live Easter without entering into the mystery. It is not something intellectual, something we only know or read about… It is more, much more!

"To enter into the mystery" means the ability to wonder, to contemplate; the ability to listen to the silence and to hear the tiny whisper amid great silence by which God speaks to us (cf 1 *Kg* 19:12).

To enter into the mystery demands that we not be afraid of reality: that we not be locked into ourselves, that we not flee from what we fail to understand, that we not close our eyes to problems or deny them, that we not dismiss our questions…

To enter into the mystery means going beyond our own comfort zone, beyond the laziness and indifference which hold us back, and going out in search of truth, beauty and love. It is seeking a deeper meaning, an answer, and not an easy one, to the questions which challenge our faith, our fidelity and our very existence.

We need to adore

To enter into the mystery, we need humility, the lowliness to abase ourselves, to come down from the pedestal of our

"I" which is so proud, of our presumption; the humility not to take ourselves so seriously, recognizing who we really are: creatures with strengths and weaknesses, sinners in need of forgiveness. To enter into the mystery we need the lowliness that is powerlessness, the renunciation of our idols... in a word, we need to adore. Without adoration, we cannot enter into the mystery.

The women who were Jesus' disciples teach us all of this. They kept watch that night, together with Mary. And she, the Virgin Mother, helped them not to lose faith and hope. As a result, they did not remain prisoners of fear and sadness, but at the first light of dawn they went out carrying their ointments, their hearts anointed with love. They went forth and found the tomb open. And they went in. They had kept watch, they went forth and they entered into the Mystery. May we learn from them to keep watch with God and with Mary our Mother, so that we too may enter into the Mystery which leads from death to life.

EASTERTIDE

EASTER SUNDAY

Light has dispelled the darkness

Jesus Christ is risen!

Love has triumphed over hatred, life has conquered death, light has dispelled the darkness!

Out of love for us, Jesus Christ stripped himself of his divine glory, emptied himself, took on the form of a slave and humbled himself even to death, death on a cross. For this reason God exalted him and made him Lord of the universe. Jesus is Lord!

By his death and resurrection, Jesus shows everyone *the way* to life and happiness: this way is *humility*, which involves *humiliation*. This is the path which leads to glory. *Only those who humble themselves can go towards the "things that are above", towards God* (cf. *Col* 3:1-4). The proud look "down from above"; the humble look "up from below".

On Easter morning, alerted by the women, Peter and John ran to the tomb. They found it open and empty. Then they drew near and *"bent down"* in order to enter it. To enter into the mystery, we need to "bend down", to abase ourselves. Only those who abase themselves understand the glorification of Jesus and are able to follow him on his way.

The seeds of another humanity

The world proposes that we put ourselves forward at all costs, that we compete, that we prevail… But Christians, by the grace of Christ, dead and risen, are *the seeds of another humanity*, in which we seek to live in service to one another, not to be arrogant, but rather respectful and ready to help.

This *is not weakness, but true strength!* Those who bear within them God's power, his love and his justice, do not need to employ violence; they speak and act with the power of truth, beauty and love.

From the risen Lord we ask today the grace not to succumb to the pride which fuels violence and war, but to have the humble courage of pardon and peace. We ask Jesus, the Victor over death, to lighten the sufferings of our many brothers and sisters who are persecuted for his name, and of all those who suffer injustice as a result of ongoing conflicts and violence. There are so many of them!

We ask for peace and freedom for the many men and women subject to old and new forms of enslavement on the part of criminal individuals and groups. Peace and liberty for the victims of drug dealers, who are often allied with the powers who ought to defend peace and harmony in the human family. And we ask peace for this world subjected to arms dealers, who profit from the blood of men and women.

May the marginalized, the imprisoned, the poor and the migrants who are so often rejected, maltreated and discarded, the sick and the suffering, children, especially those who are victims of violence; all who today are in mourning, and all men and women of goodwill, hear the consoling and healing voice of the Lord Jesus: "Peace to you!" (*Lk* 24:36). "Fear not, for I am risen and I shall always be with you" (cf. Roman Missal, Entrance Antiphon for Easter Day).

Easter Monday

Jesus is risen!

On this Easter Monday the Gospel (cf. *Mt* 28:8-15) presents to us the narrative of the women who, on arriving at Jesus' tomb, find it empty and see an Angel who announces to them that he is risen. And as they run to tell this news to the disciples, they encounter Jesus himself who says to them: "Go and tell my brethren to go to Galilee, and there they will see me" (v. 10). Galilee is the "periphery" where Jesus began his preaching; and from there he will share the Gospel of the Resurrection, for it to be proclaimed to all, and that everyone might encounter him, the Risen One, present and working in history. Today too he is with us, here in the Square.

This, therefore, is the proclamation that the Church repeats from the first day: "*Christ is risen!*". And, in him, through Baptism, we too are risen, we have passed from death to life, from the slavery of sin to the freedom of love. Behold the Good News that we are called to take to others and to every place, inspired by the Holy Spirit. Faith in the Resurrection of Jesus and the hope that he brought us is the most beautiful gift that the Christian can and must give to his brothers. To all and to each, therefore, let us not tire of saying: Christ is risen! Let us repeat it all together, today here in the Square: Christ is risen! Let us repeat it with words, but above all with the witness of our lives. The happy news of the Resurrection should shine on our faces, in our feelings and attitudes, in the way we treat others.

We proclaim the Resurrection of Christ when his light illuminates the dark moments of our life and we can share that with others: when we know how to smile with those who smile and weep with those who weep; when we walk beside those who are sad and in danger of losing hope; when we recount our experience of faith with those who are searching for meaning and for happiness. With our attitude, with our witness, with our life, we say: Jesus is risen! Let us say it with all our soul.

A reflection of Mary's joy

We are in days of the Easter Octave, during which the joyful atmosphere of the Resurrection accompanies us. It's curious how the Liturgy considers the entire Octave as one single day, in order to help us centre into the Mystery, so that his grace may impress itself on our hearts and our lives. Easter is the event that brought radical news for every human being, for history and for the world: the triumph of life over death; it is the feast of reawakening and of rebirth. Let us allow our lives to be conquered and transformed by the Resurrection!

Let us ask the Virgin Mother, the silent witness of the death and Resurrection of her Son, to foster the growth of

Paschal joy in us. Let us do it now with the recitation of the Regina Caeli, which in the Easter Season substitutes the prayer of the Angelus. In this prayer, expressed by the Alleluia, we turn to Mary inviting her to rejoice, because the One whom she carried in her womb is risen as he promised, and we entrust ourselves to her intercession. In fact, our joy is a reflection of Mary's joy, for it is she who guarded and guards with faith the events of Jesus. Let us therefore recite this prayer with the emotion of children who are happy because their mother is happy.

SECOND SUNDAY OF EASTER
Touching the Paschal Mystery

Today is the eighth day after Easter, and the Gospel according to John documents for us the two appearances of the Risen Jesus to the Apostles gathered in the Upper Room, where on the evening of Easter Thomas was absent, and eight days later, he was present. The first time, the Lord showed them the wounds to his body, breathed on them and said: "As the Father has sent me, even so I send you" (*Jn* 20:21). He imparts his same mission, through the power of the Holy Spirit.

But that night Thomas, who did not want to believe what the others witnessed, was not there. "Unless I see in his hands the print of the nails, and place my finger in the mark of the nails, and place my hand in his side", he said, "I will not believe" (cf. *Jn* 20:25). Eight days later - which is precisely today - Jesus returned to stand among them and turned immediately to Thomas, inviting him to touch the wounds in his hands and his side. He faced his incredulity so that, through the signs of the passion, he was able to reach the fullness of faith in the Paschal Mystery, namely faith in the Resurrection of Jesus.

Thomas was one who was not satisfied and seeks, intending to confirm himself, to have his own personal experience. After initial resistance and apprehension, in the end even he was able to believe, even though through effort, he came to believe. Jesus waited for him patiently and offered himself to the difficulties and uncertainty of the last to arrive. The Lord proclaimed "blessed", those who believe without seeing (cf. v. 29) the first of which is Mary his Mother. He also met the needs of the doubting disciple: "Put your finger here, and see my hands…" (v. 27). In the redeeming contact with the wounds of the Risen One, Thomas showed his own wounds, his own injuries, his own lacerations, his own humiliation; in the print of the nails he found the decisive proof that he was loved, that he was expected, that he was understood. He found himself before the Messiah filled with kindness, mercy, tenderness. This was the Lord he was searching for, he, in the hidden depths of his being, for he had always known the Lord was like this. And how many of us are searching deep in our heart to meet Jesus, just as he is: kind, merciful, tender! For we know, deep down, that he is like this. Having rediscovered personal contact with Christ who is amiable and mercifully patient, Thomas understood the profound significance of his Resurrection and, intimately transformed, he declared his full and total faith in him exclaiming: "My Lord and my God!" (v. 28). Beautiful, Thomas' expression is beautiful!

He was able to "touch" the Paschal Mystery which fully demonstrated God's redeeming love (cf. *Ep* 2:4). All of us too are like Thomas: on this second Sunday of Easter we are called to contemplate, in the wounds of the Risen One, Divine Mercy, which overcomes all human limitations and shines on the darkness of evil and of sin.

THIRD SUNDAY OF EASTER

See, recall and tell

In the Bible Readings of today's liturgy the word "witnesses" is mentioned twice. The first time it is on the lips of Peter who, after the healing of the paralytic at the Door of the Temple of Jerusalem, exclaims: You "killed the Author of life, whom God raised from the dead. To this we are witnesses" (*Ac* 3:15). The second time it is on the lips of the Risen Jesus. On the evening of Easter he opens the minds of the disciples to the mystery of his death and Resurrection, saying to them: "You are witnesses to these things" (*Lk* 24:48). The Apostles, who saw the Risen Christ with their own eyes, could not keep silent about their extraordinary experience. He had shown himself to them so that the truth of his Resurrection would reach everyone by way of their witness. The Church has the duty to continue this mission over time. Every baptised person is called to bear witness, with their life and words, that Jesus is Risen, that Jesus is alive and present among us. We are all called to testify that Jesus is alive.

We may ask ourselves: who is a witness? A witness is a person who has seen, who recalls and tells. *See*, *recall* and *tell*: these are three verbs which describe the identity and mission. A witness is a person who *has seen* with an objective eye, has seen reality, but not with an indifferent eye; he has seen and has let himself become involved in the event. For this reason, one *recalls*, not only because she knows how to reconstruct the events exactly but also because those facts spoke to her and she grasped their profound meaning. Then a witness *tells*, not in a cold and detached way but as one who has allowed himself to be called into question and from that day changed the way of life. A witness is someone who has changed his or her life.

A real event

The content of Christian witness is not a theory, it's not an ideology or a complex system of precepts and prohibitions or a moralist theory, but a message of salvation, a real event, rather a Person: it is the Risen Christ, the living and only Saviour of all. He can be testified to by those who have personal experience of him, in prayer and in the Church, through a journey that has its foundation in Baptism, its nourishment in the Eucharist, its seal in Confirmation, its continual conversion in Penitence. Thanks to this journey, ever guided by the Word of God, every Christian can become a witness of the Risen Jesus. And his or her witness is all the more credible, the more it shines through a life lived by the Gospel, a joyful, courageous, gentle peaceful, merciful life. Instead, if a Christian gives in to ease, vanity, selfishness, if he or she becomes deaf and blind to the question of "resurrection" of many brothers and sisters, how can he or she communicate the living Jesus, how can the Christian communicate the freeing power of the living Jesus and his infinite tenderness?

May Mary our Mother sustain us by her intercession, that we might become, with all our limitations but by the grace of faith, witnesses of the Risen Lord, bringing the Paschal gifts of joy and peace to the people we encounter.

FOURTH SUNDAY OF EASTER
The true and good shepherd

This day, the Fourth Sunday of Easter, called "Good Shepherd Sunday", invites us each year to rediscover, with ever new astonishment, how Jesus defined himself, reading it again in the light of his passion, death and resurrection. "The good shepherd lays down his life for the sheep" (*Jn* 10:11): these words are wholly fulfilled when Christ, freely obeying the will of the Father, is immolated on the Cross. The significance that he is "the good shepherd" thus becomes completely clear: he gives life, he offered his life in sacrifice for us all: for you, for you, for you, for me, for everyone! And for this reason he is the good shepherd!

Christ is the true shepherd, who fulfils the loftiest model of love for the flock: he freely *lays down* his own life, no one takes it from him (cf. v. 18), but he *gives* it for the sheep (v. 17). In open opposition to false shepherds, Jesus presents himself as the one true shepherd of the people. A bad pastor thinks of himself and exploits the sheep; a good shepherd thinks of the sheep and gives himself. Unlike the mercenary, Christ the pastor is a careful guide who participates in the life of his flock, does not seek other interests, has no ambition other than guiding, feeding and protecting his sheep. All of this at the highest price, that of sacrificing his own life.

The providence of God

In the figure of Jesus, the Good Shepherd, we contemplate the providence of God, his paternal solicitude for each one of us. He does not leave us on our own! The result of this contemplation of Jesus the true and good shepherd, is the exclamation of poignant astonishment that we find in the Second Reading of the day's Liturgy: "See what love the Father has given us…" (1 *Jn* 3:1). It is truly a surprising and mysterious love, for by giving us Jesus as the shepherd who gives his life for us, the Father has given us all of the greatest and most precious that he could give us. It is the purest and most sublime love, for it is not motivated by necessity, is not conditioned on accounting, is not attracted by a self-interested desire for exchange. Before this love of God, we feel immense joy and we open ourselves to recognizing how much we have freely received.

But it is not enough to contemplate and give thanks. It is also necessary to *follow* the good shepherd. In particular, those whose mission is to be a guide in the Church - priests, bishops, popes - are called to take on not the mentality of manager but that of *servant*, in imitation of Jesus who, in emptying himself, saved us with his mercy.

FIFTH SUNDAY OF EASTER

Abide in me

Something Jesus often repeats, especially during the Last Supper, is: "Abide in me". Do not tire of me, abide in me. And Christian life is precisely this: to abide in Jesus. This is Christian life: to abide in Jesus. And Jesus, in order to explain to us what he means by this, uses this beautiful figure of the vine: "I am the true vine, you the branches" (cf. *Jn* 15:1). And every branch that is not joined to the vine ends up dying, it bears no fruit; and then is thrown away to feed the fire. Many are used for this, to feed the fire - they are very, very useful - but not in bearing fruit. Rather, the branches that are united to the vine receive the lifeblood and thus develop, grow and bear fruit. It's a simple, simple image. To abide in Jesus means to be united to him in order to receive life from him, love from him; the Holy Spirit from him. It's true, we are all sinners, but if we abide in Jesus, like the branches to the vine, the Lord comes. He prunes us a little, so that we can bear more fruit. He always takes care of us. But if we detach from him, if we do not abide in the Lord, we are Christians in name only, but not in life; we are Christians, but dead ones, because we bear no fruit, like branches broken away from the vine.

To abide in Jesus means to be willing to receive life from him, as well as pardon, even pruning, but to receive it from him. To abide in Jesus means to seek Jesus, to pray, prayer. To abide in Jesus means to approach the sacraments: the Eucharist, Reconciliation. To abide in Jesus - and this is the most difficult thing - means to do what Jesus did, to have the same attitude as Jesus. But when we "slur" someone else [speaking badly of others], for example, or when we gossip, we do not abide in Jesus. Jesus never did this. When we are liars, we do not abide in Jesus. He never did this. When we cheat others with the dirty deals that are available to everyone, we are dead branches, we do not abide in Jesus. To abide in Jesus is to do the things that he did: to do good, to help others, to pray to the Father, to care for the sick, to help the poor, to have the joy of the Holy Spirit.

Do I abide in Jesus?

A beautiful question for us Christians is this: do I abide in Jesus or am I far from Jesus? Am I united to the vine that gives me life or am I a dead branch, that is incapable of bearing fruit, giving witness? And there are other branches too, of which Jesus does not speak here, but he speaks about them elsewhere: those who make themselves look like disciples of Jesus, but they do the opposite of Jesus' disciple: these are hypocritical branches. Perhaps they go to Mass every Sunday, perhaps their face looks like a holy card, all pious, but then they live like pagans. And Jesus calls them hypocrites in the Gospel. Jesus is good, he invites us to abide in him. He gives us the strength, and if we slide into sin - we are all sinners - he forgives us, because he is merciful. But what he wants are these two things: that we abide in him and that we are not hypocrites. And with this a Christian life moves forward.

And what does the Lord give us if we abide in him? We just heard it: "If you abide in me, and my words abide in you, ask whatever you will, and it shall be done for you" (*Jn* 15:7). The power of prayer: "Ask whatever you will", that is, prayer is so powerful that Jesus does whatever we ask of him. However if our prayer is weak - if it is not done sincerely in Jesus - prayer does not bear its fruit, because the branch is not united to the vine. But if the branch is united to the vine, that is, "if you abide in me and my words abide in you, ask whatever you will, and it shall be done for you". And this is the almighty prayer. Where does the omnipotence of this prayer come from? From abiding in Jesus; from being united to Jesus, like the branch to the vine. May the Lord grant us this grace.

You are the branches

Today's Gospel shows us Jesus during the Last Supper, in the moment he knows his death is close at hand. His 'hour' has come. For it is the last time he is with his disciples, and now he wants to impress firmly a fundamental truth in their minds: even when he will no longer be physically present in the midst of them, they will still be able to remain *united to him in a new way*, and thus bear much fruit. Everyone can be united to Jesus in a new way. If, on the contrary, one should lose this unity with him, this union with him, would become sterile, or rather, harmful to the community. And to express this reality, this new way of being united to him, Jesus uses the image of the vine and the branches: Just "as a branch cannot bear fruit by itself, unless it abides in the vine, neither can you, unless you abide in me. I am the vine, you are the branches" (*Jn* 15:4-5). With this image he teaches us how to abide him, to be united to him, even though he is not physically present.

Jesus is the vine, and through him - like the sap in the tree - the *very love of God, the Holy Spirit* is passed to the branches. Look: we are the branches, and through this parable, Jesus wants us to understand the importance of remaining united to him. The branches are not self-sufficient, but depend totally on the vine, in which the source of their life is found. So it is with us Christians. Grafted by Baptism in Christ, we have freely received the gift of new life from him; and thanks to the Church we are able to remain in vital communion with Christ. We must remain faithful to Baptism, and grow in intimacy with the Lord through prayer, listening and docility to his Word - read the Gospel - participation in the Sacraments, especially the Eucharist and Reconciliation.

The gifts of the Holy Spirit

When one is intimately united to Jesus, he enjoys the gifts of the Holy Spirit, which are - as St Paul tells us - "love, joy, peace, patience, kindness, generosity, faithfulness, gentleness, self-control" (*Gal* 5:22). These are the gifts that we receive if we remain united in Jesus; and therefore a person who is so united in him does so much good for neighbour and society, is a Christian person. In fact, one is recognized as a true Christian by this attitude, as a tree is recognized by its fruit. The fruits of this profound union with Christ are wonderful: our whole person is transformed by the grace of the Spirit: soul, understanding, will, affections, and even body, because we are united body and soul. We receive a new way of being, the life of Christ becomes our own: we are able to think like him, to act like him, to see the world and the things in it with the eyes of Jesus. And so we are able to love our brothers, beginning with the poorest and those who suffer the most, as he did and love them with his heart, and so bear fruits of goodness, of charity, and of peace in the world.

Each one of us is a branch of the one vine; and all of us together are called to bear the fruits of this common membership in Christ and in the Church. Let us entrust ourselves to the intercession of the Virgin Mary, so that we might be able to be living branches in the Church and witness to our faith in a consistent manner - consistency of one's own life and thought, of life and faith - knowing that all of us, according to our particular vocations, participate in the one saving mission of Christ.

SIXTH SUNDAY OF EASTER

Jesus shows us the path of love

Today's Gospel - John, Chapter 15 - brings us back to the Last Supper, when we hear Jesus' new commandment. He says: "This is my commandment, that you love one another as I have loved you" (v. 12). Thinking of his imminent sacrifice on the cross, he adds: "Greater love has no man than this, that a man lay down his life for his friends. You are my friends, if you do what I command you" (v. 13-14). These words, said at the Last Supper, summarize Jesus' full message. Actually they summarize all that he did: Jesus gave his life for his friends. Friends who did not understand him, in fact they abandoned, betrayed and denied him at the crucial moment. This tells us that he loves us, even though we don't deserve his love. Jesus loves us in this way!

Thus Jesus *shows us the path* to follow him: the path of love. His commandment is not a simple teaching which is always abstract or foreign to life. Christ's commandment is *new* because he realized it first, he gave his flesh and thus the law of love is written upon the heart of man (cf. *Jer* 31:33). And how is it written? It is written with the fire of the Holy Spirit. With this Spirit that Jesus gives us, we too can take this path!

It is a real path, a path that leads us to come out of ourselves and go towards others. Jesus showed us that the love of God *is realized in love for our neighbour*. Both go hand-in-hand. The pages of the Gospel are full of this love: adults and children, educated and uneducated, rich and poor, just and sinners all were welcomed into the heart of Christ.

Small and great actions

Therefore, this Word of God calls us to love one another, even if we do not always understand each other, and do not always get along...it is then that Christian love is seen. A love which manifests even if there are differences of opinion or character. Love is greater than these differences! This is the love that Jesus taught us. It is a new love because Jesus and his Spirit renewed it. It is a *redeeming love, free from selfishness*. A love which *gives our hearts joy,* as Jesus himself said: "These things I have spoken to you, that my joy may be in you, and that your joy may be full" (*Jn* 15:11).

It is precisely Christ's love that the Holy Spirit pours into our hearts to make everyday wonders in the Church and in the world. There are many *small and great actions* which obey the Lord's commandment: "Love one another as I have loved you" (cf. *Jn* 15:12). Small everyday *actions*, *actions* of closeness to an elderly person, to a child, to a sick person, to a lonely person, those in difficulty, without a home, without work, an immigrant, a refugee…. Thanks to the strength of the Word of Christ, each one of us can make ourselves the brother or sister of those whom we encounter. Actions of closeness, actions which manifest the love that Christ taught us.

May our Most Holy Mother help us in this, so that in each of our daily lives love of God and love of neighbour may be ever united.

SEVENTH SUNDAY OF EASTER
Sowing the seeds of unity

The Acts of the Apostles have set before us the early Church as she elects the man whom God called to take the place of Judas in the college of the Apostles. It is has to do not with a job, but with service. Indeed, Matthias, on whom the choice falls, receives a mission which Peter defines in these words: "One of these men…must become a witness with us to his resurrection", the resurrection of Christ (*Ac* 1:21-23). In this way Peter sums up what it means to be part of the Twelve: it means to be *a witness to Jesus' resurrection*. The fact that he says "with us" brings us to realize that the mission of proclaiming the risen Christ is not an individual undertaking: it is to be carried out in common, with the apostolic college and with the community. The Apostles had a direct and overwhelming experience of the resurrection; they were eyewitnesses to that event. Thanks to their authoritative testimony, many people came to believe; from faith in the risen Lord, Christian communities were born and are born continually. We too, today, base our faith in the risen Lord on the witness of the Apostles, which has come down to us through the mission of the Church. Our faith is firmly

linked to their testimony, as to an unbroken chain which
spans the centuries, made up not only by the successors
of the Apostles, but also by succeeding generations
of Christians. Like the Apostles, each one of Christ's
followers is called to become a witness to his resurrection,
above all in those human settings where forgetfulness of
God and human disorientation are most evident.

If this is to happen, we need to *remain in the risen
Christ and in his love*, as the First Letter of Saint John
has reminded us: "He who abides in love abides in God,
and God abides in him" (*1 Jn* 4:16). Jesus had repeated
insistently to his disciples: "Abide in me... Abide in my
love" (*Jn* 15:4, 9). This is the secret of the saints: abiding
in Christ, joined to him like branches to the vine, in order
to bear much fruit (cf. *Jn* 15:1-8). And this fruit is none
other than love.

Abiding in love

*A relationship with the risen Jesus is - so to speak - the
"atmosphere" in which Christians live*, and in which they
find the strength to remain faithful to the Gospel, even
amid obstacles and misunderstandings. "Abiding in love."

An essential aspect of witness to the risen Lord is *unity
among ourselves, his disciples*, in the image of his own
unity with the Father. Today too, in the Gospel, we heard
Jesus' prayer on the eve of his passion: "that they may be
one, even as we are one" (*Jn* 17:11). From this eternal love

between the Father and the Son, poured into our hearts through the Holy Spirit (cf. *Rm* 5:5), our mission and our fraternal communion draw strength; this love is the ever-flowing source of our joy in following the Lord along the path of his poverty, his virginity and his obedience; and this same love calls us to cultivate contemplative prayer.

To abide in God and in his love, and thus to proclaim by our words and our lives the resurrection of Jesus, to live in unity with one another and with charity towards all. How do I bear witness to the risen Christ? This is a question we have to ask ourselves. How do I abide in him? How do I dwell in his love? Am I capable of "sowing" in my family, in my workplace and in my community, the seed of that unity which he has bestowed on us by giving us a share in the life of the Trinity?

When we return home today, let us take with us the joy of this encounter with the risen Lord. Let us cultivate in our hearts the commitment to abide in God's love. Let us remain united to him and among ourselves, and follow in the footsteps of these four women, models of sanctity whom the Church invites us to imitate.

PENTECOST

Strengthened by the Spirit

"As the Father has sent me, even so I send you… Receive the Holy Spirit" (*Jn* 20:21-22); this is what Jesus says to us. The gift of the Spirit on the evening of the Resurrection took place once again on the day of Pentecost, intensified this time by extraordinary outward signs. On the evening of Easter, Jesus appeared to the Apostles and breathed on them his Spirit (cf. *Jn* 20:22); on the morning of Pentecost the outpouring occurred in a resounding way, like a wind which shook the place the Apostles were in, filling their minds and hearts. They received a new strength so great that they were able to proclaim Christ's Resurrection in different languages: "They were all filled with the Holy Spirit, and began to speak in other tongues, as the Spirit gave them utterance" (*Ac* 2:4). Together with them was Mary, the Mother of Jesus, the first disciple, there too as Mother of the nascent Church. With her peace, with her smile, with her maternity, she accompanied the joyful young Bride, the Church of Jesus.

The word of God, especially in today's readings, tells us that the Spirit is at work in individuals and communities filled with himself; the Spirit makes them capable of *recipere*

Deum [receiving God], *capax Dei* [with the capacity for God], as the holy Church Fathers say. And what does the Holy Spirit do with this new capability which he gives us? *He guides us into all the truth* (cf. *Jn*16:13), *he renews the face of the earth* (*Ps* 103:30), and *he gives us his fruits* (cf. *Gal* 5:22-23). He guides, he renews and he makes fruitful.

In the Gospel, Jesus promises his disciples that, when he has returned to the Father, the Holy Spirit will come to guide them into all the truth (cf. *Jn* 16:13). Indeed he calls the Holy Spirit "the Spirit of truth", and explains to his disciples that the Spirit will bring them to understand ever more clearly what he, the Messiah, has said and done, especially in regard to his death and resurrection. To the Apostles, who could not bear the scandal of their Master's sufferings, the Spirit would give a new understanding of the truth and beauty of that saving event. At first they were paralyzed with fear, shut in the Upper Room to avoid the aftermath of Good Friday. Now they would no longer be ashamed to be Christ's disciples; they would no longer tremble before the courts of men. Filled with the Holy Spirit, they would now understand "all the truth": that the death of Jesus was not his defeat, but rather the ultimate expression of God's love, a love that, in the Resurrection, conquers death and exalts Jesus as the Living One, the Lord, the Redeemer of mankind, the Lord of history and of the world. This truth, to which the Apostles were witnesses, became Good News, to be proclaimed to all.

The Holy Spirit renews the earth

Then the Holy Spirit renews - guides and renews - *renews the earth*. The Psalmist says: "You send forth your Spirit… and you renew the face of the earth" (*Ps* 103:30). The account of the birth of the Church in the Acts of the Apostles is significantly linked to this Psalm, which is a great hymn of praise to God the Creator. The Holy Spirit whom Christ sent from the Father, and the Creator Spirit who gives life to all things, are one and the same. Respect for creation, then, is a requirement of our faith: the "garden" in which we live is not entrusted to us to be exploited, but rather to be cultivated and tended with respect (cf. *Gn* 2:15). Yet this is possible only if Adam - the man formed from the earth - allows himself in turn to be renewed by the Holy Spirit, only if he allows himself to be re-formed by the Father on the model of Christ, the new Adam. In this way, renewed by the Spirit, we will indeed be able to experience the freedom of the sons and daughters, in harmony with all creation. In every creature we will be able to see reflected the glory of the Creator, as another Psalm says: "How great is your name, O Lord our God, through all the earth!" (*Ps* 8:2, 10). He guides, he renews and he gives; he gives fruits.

In the Letter to the Galatians, Saint Paul wants to show the "fruits" manifested in the lives of those who walk in the way of the Spirit (cf. *Ga* 5:22). On the one hand, he presents "the flesh", with its list of attendant vices: the works of selfish people closed to God. On the other hand, there are those who by faith allow the Spirit of God to break into their lives. In them, God's gifts blossom, summed up in nine joyful virtues which Paul calls "fruits of the Spirit". Hence his appeal, at the start and the end of the reading, as a programme for life: "Walk by the Spirit" (*Ga* 5:6, 25).

The gifts of the Holy Spirit

The world needs men and women who are not closed in on themselves, but filled with the Holy Spirit. Closing oneself off from the Holy Spirit means not only a lack of freedom; it is a sin. There are many ways one can close oneself off to the Holy Spirit: by selfishness for one's own gain; by rigid legalism - seen in the attitude of the doctors of the law to whom Jesus referred as "hypocrites"; by neglect of what Jesus taught; by living the Christian life not as service to others but in the pursuit of personal interests; and in so many other ways. However, the world needs the courage, hope, faith and perseverance of Christ's followers. The world needs the fruits, the gifts of the Holy Spirit, as Saint Paul lists them: "love, joy, peace, patience, kindness, goodness, faithfulness, gentleness, self-control" (*Ga* 5:22). The gift of the Holy Spirit has been bestowed upon the Church and upon each one of us, so that we may live lives of genuine faith and active charity, that we may sow the seeds of reconciliation and peace. Strengthened by the Spirit - who guides, who guides us into the truth, who renews us and the whole earth, and who gives us his fruits - strengthened in the Spirit and by these many gifts, may we be able to battle uncompromisingly against sin, to battle uncompromisingly against corruption, which continues to spread in the world day after day, by devoting ourselves with patient perseverance to the works of justice and peace.

Sources

This booklet draws together homilies, General Audiences, Angelus, Regina Caeli and Urbi et Orbi addresses given by Pope Francis which took place in Rome between 18th February 2015 and 24th May 2015.

Homily for Blessing and Imposition of Ashes, Wednesday, 18th February 2015

Angelus, First Sunday of Lent, 22nd February 2015

Angelus, Second Sunday of Lent, 1st March 2015

Angelus, Third Sunday of Lent, 8th March 2015

Homily, Third Sunday of Lent, 8th March 2015

Homily, Penitential Celebration, Friday, 13th March 2015

Angelus, Fourth Sunday of Lent, 15th March 2015

Angelus, Fifth Sunday of Lent, 22nd March 2015

Homily, Palm Sunday, 29th March 2015

General Audience, Wednesday, 1st April 2015

Holy Chrism Mass, Holy Thursday, 2nd April 2015

Homily, Holy Thursday, 2nd April 2015 (Mass of the Lord's Supper)

Homily, Holy Saturday, 4th April 2015

Urbi et Orbi - Easter Sunday, 5th April 2015

Regina Caeli, Easter Monday, 6th April 2015

Regina Caeli, Second Sunday of Easter (or Divine Mercy Sunday), 12th April 2015

Regina Caeli, Third Sunday of Easter, 19th April 2015

Regina Caeli, Fourth Sunday of Easter, 26th April 2015

Regina Caeli, Fifth Sunday of Easter, 3rd May 2015

Homily, Fifth Sunday of Easter, 3rd May 2015

Regina Caeli, Sixth Sunday of Easter, 10th May 2015

Homily, Seventh Sunday of Easter, 17th May 2015

Homily, Solemnity of Pentecost, Sunday, 24th May 2015